Prosperous Me

Accepting The Bounty Of Your Birthright!

Michelle Wadleigh

Bruce Daniels

Prosperous Me, Accepting the Bounty of your Birthright!

DEDICATION

These few yet powerful pages of treatments and
wisdom are dedicated to YOU, to the prosperous and abundant you,
to the you who has finally said *enough!*,
I'm done living with lack. I now accept my Divine Birthright!

This book is dedicated to RELIGIOUS SCIENTISTS, old and new.
Yes, Religious Scientists, and Divine Scientists, and practicing
Unity people, and any other New Thought/Metaphysical students.

I will not spare the metaphysical jargon, or try to explain what I
mean, or use language accepted by the dictionary.

This book is dedicated to the *Beingness* and the *Allness* of YOU, to
the non-local you, and to the consciousness of this world. Because
as we who function in consciousness all know, we are part of this
organism called Life, God, Spirit, Energy. There is no
private good. When any one of us prospers,
we all grow and prosper together.

*Here is to you as the perfectly natural prosperous being that you are
as you accept your Divine Birthright!*

LET'S RISE TOGETHER!

Forward by John Randolph Price

In this practical and easy to read book, Michelle Wadleigh charts a course of instruction based on her own intuitive understanding of the secrets of a life more abundant. Included is the Truth that whatever we are seeking, we already have, that nothing deemed *good* is ever missing in our lives unless it is denied mentally and emotionally.

In her own method of demonstrating the power of manifestation, Michelle draws on the energies of inspiration, love, joy, and faith, which lead to a heart-mind connection in tune with our Divine Self. To complete the process she offers three steps to follow for each day: An activity to *Practice,* a *Quote* from a spiritual teacher, and an *Affirmation of Gratitude.*
She shows us that it is not only good to be rich, but is our Divine Right to enjoy abundant prosperity.
This is a book that produces richest blessings.

Enjoy!

INTRODUCTION

This book is written to be pure in its intention. That intention is Spiritual Mind Treatment and Affirmative Prayer married with some wisdom and practical application. It's not my intention to replace any of the works of the masters but to offer you something that works in conjunction with your favorites: Napoleon Hill, Edwene Gaines, Catherine Ponder, Mary Morrissey, Bob Proctor, Wallace Wattles, John Randolph Price and so many more. Work their programs, yes, but every night read along with the treatments in this text. These treatments are written to be bold and to shake you up in your comfort zone, never making any excuses for being a fully prosperous being.

I'll always remember the first time I read, *The Science of Getting Rich* where Wallace Wattles reminds us: "It is perfectly right that you should desire to be rich; if you are a normal man or woman you cannot help doing so. It is perfectly right that you should give your best attention to the science of getting rich, for it is the noblest and most necessary of all studies. If you neglect this study, you are derelict in your duty to yourself, to God and humanity; for you can render to God and humanity no greater service then to make the most of yourself." After all, the richer you are, the more you can tithe, right?

Begin here with the purity of our teaching. Let's use what we know. If you feel blocked, do the other work you know is necessary. We are not trying to do it all here in this book. If your flow is blocked, you probably need to do some forgiveness work. Buy *Radical Forgiveness* by Colin Tipping; it's the best work on the subject (in my humble opinion). Still blocked? Buy *Dark Side of the Light Chasers* by Debbie Ford and *do* some shadow work. (Definitely work along with a Shadow Coach; this work opens all sorts of stuff.) Can't figure it out on your own? Use a practitioner or prayer chaplain; that's what they are there for, that's why they've trained so hard. And don't go it alone, use this with your prayer partner or with a mastermind group. Remember, "Wherever two or more are gathered ...."

Let those of us who are reading these treatments be willing to accept our good and our greater good without excuses. Remember, there is no private good. As you begin to lift your consciousness, others will follow from your inspiration and example. Someone must be willing to be brilliant and hold the light for others. Let it be you. In Truth, there is no reason that it cannot be YOU.

LET'S DEMONSTRATE THE TEACHING TOGETHER, POWERFULLY!

The opportunity for self-expression and compensation is always open to me and I am at all times compelled to know, accept and operate upon this opportunity. I have abundance because I am abundance. All that the Father hath is mine.
Ernest Holmes

The spiritual substance from which comes all visible wealth is never depleted. It is right with you are all the time and responds to your faith in it and your demands on it.
Charles Fillmore

To Begin . . .

This book is written for a 31-day month so you don't run out of treatments before a month runs out of days. You have a daily reader for a solid month.

Consider these things when reading this book:

- It is great to have your first thought of the day to be empowering to set your mood, so consider reaching for a treatment before you step out of bed.
- It is also good to lay your head on the pillow at night with something uplifting and empowering as the last thought to take into your sleep. Take these words *into* your dreams.
- Read aloud whenever possible, or try recording your own voice so you can listen to it in the car or before you sleep at night.
- Act faithfully.
- Make good and intelligent financial decisions. You don't prove you are rich by buying on credit. If you don't have the money, wait until you do.
- Treat AND move your feet.
- Remember consciousness first, consciousness always.
- Lastly, you cannot out-demonstrate your consciousness. Your work is to expand your consciousness first, all else will follow.

Feel free to begin this book on any day of the month and remember to use it over and over again.
If you really want to receive its full bounty, take time after reading each treatment to meditate for at least fifteen minutes to allow the word to settle deeply into your consciousness.
Keep fresh your realizations by journaling what comes.

Dear Spirit,

    Today, _October 1st 2016_, I begin my thirty-one day practice setting the intention to read every word aloud at least three times a day; upon waking in the morning, mid-day to noon and before I sleep at night.

    I commit to writing in my journal, to staying awake and to catching all erroneous and limiting thoughts that have kept me limited in my prosperity.

    I commit to opening my mind and my heart to allow the Allness of Spirit to be that which informs my behavior, my thinking and my decision making.

    I live, expecting good, expecting the world to work and expecting my prosperity to grow and multiply as naturally as any seed, planted in fertile soil grows freely.

    I promise to share what I've learned and to support others in accepting their Divine Birthright of prosperity.

With my love from my Prosperous Me self,

_____

Date _____ 10/1/16 _____

Day 1
Treatment

Today is the day I resurrect myself. I rise above the old ways of thinking and being to recreate myself in a way that I am recognized from afar as a woman/man of means, as a woman/man of abundance, as a woman/man who knows prosperity intimately.
Today I begin my journey in a new direction and take on the thinking and the habits that accompany individuals who know success as their identity. As of today, my identity will be recognized in this way: SUCCESSFUL, PROSPEROUS, ABUNDANT, STEADY, ALIVE and VITAL.

I am seen and recognized this way. I recognize and see myself this way. I expect myself to do everything required to grow my field of consciousness regarding prosperity and abundance. I expect this movement to be easy and in total alignment with my goal of raising my income dramatically. This is the day that Spirit has made, and it is a good and glorious day.
And so it is!

Practice
Today I commit to reading my prosperity treatments daily, morning and night, and to repeating the gratitude affirmation throughout the day.

Quote
The person who stops studying merely because he has finished school is forever hopelessly doomed to mediocrity, no matter what may be his calling.

Napoleon Hill

Affirmation of Gratitude
I am grateful for my prosperity in its current form, as it is NOW!

Prosperous Me, Accepting the Bounty of your Birthright!

Lyft rides have been abundant oct.
$3.00 Tips $10.75 cleaners $13.00 Gas   Nov.
$4.10 coffee $.50 Racing $7.57 Supplies $20.82 food
$36.00 Alterations $9.00 CarWsh (Dec.) $18.00 Tips $11.70 Gas
$6.30 food $1.95 coffee $5.53 Supplies $14.25 cleaners

Remember to say thank you to everyone you know.

I ACCEPT MY GOOD AND MY GREATER GOOD

Cultivating a consciousness of Acceptance is critical to one who has not known it as a way of life. In many cultures and by means of religions we are taught the virtues of the meek and the impoverished as a badge of honor and adherence. In many ways we often do not feel deserving of our good and turn away from our good because of our religious indoctrination and numerous unconscious reasons, but none of them is founded in Truth.

We have received numerous contrary messages from different sources, and few of them have been supportive of our highest good or empowering in any way. Some of these messages regarding our sense of deserving is linked to the way we look, how smart we are and where we were born. Rarely is anyone taught that you deserve your full measure of good simply because you are a divine manifestation of the One, except in homes where metaphysics and ancient wisdom are taught. Most of the time, the messages support an idea of being less than, not deserving and not enough. Bah, humbug!

Enough with the lies, with the spell that has been cast, cultivated and supported by those who can't see past their conditioning to their own dominion over all things that are good.

Well, there is a new message and I am not the first one to say it but it cannot be spoken enough, and it is: **You deserve your own full measure of good. It is your Divine Birthright to be happy, healthy, joyous, fully expressed and prosperous. You deserve this not because you were born any particular color, into any particular religion, live in a wealthy town, or have received a scholarly education. You don't deserve it because society owes you, because you are a "good girl," or because God shines upon special people. You deserve your good because you are good, you are the result of good, and you deserve as much access to this possibility as anyone, anytime, anywhere.**

Here are valuable questions to ask yourself: are you ready to accept your portion of good? Are you ready to accept more than you think you deserve? Are you willing to ready yourself to accept your

good and your greater good? Are you? Really? Pay attention now, because the messages are subtle and are hiding behind all sorts of other ideas.

If you are ready, great! Reading the treatments in this text will open you up to good in ways you would have never expected. If you aren't sure yet, then make sure you read each and every treatment in this text over and over again, slowly, mindfully, and pay close attention to any messages that come up that might stand in the way. Remember to say to those messages: *This is not my truth.*

Know this:

My Truth takes me places that are new, masterful, and life-transforming. My Truth is the Truth of the One which knows me intimately as an individual worthy of all good, all the time. My Truth lifts and transforms me each and every day, and I am available to this transformed experience. This Truth knows for me things I haven't yet known for myself. It is not based on logic other than I Am. This Truth is the Truth of God, Love, Intelligence, and Life. It is a good and glorious truth, and it is My Truth NOW.

No longer shall you wait for some kind of Divine Intervention. Instead, by the words of your mouth, the readiness of your heart, and the intelligence that is you, you will stand in a stature that says YES. I am here on this plane of existence as a spiritual human. I deserve my good, and I accept my good, now.

Daily, repeat over and over again until you feel it in every cell of your being:

I ACCEPT MY GOOD AND MY GREATER GOOD.

Say this with great faith and conviction.

Day 2
Treatment

There is one loving, powerful, and creative Intelligence which knows itself as me right now. Wherever I am, I am open and fully available to It without reservation. This is my truth today and always. Wherever I am, whatever I am doing, I am always one with this One Source of my supply. Knowing that I am always surrounded by Truth, I call into my experience a life that is easy and graceful.

Everything about my life unfolds with such grace that it constantly reminds me of the abundant universe in which I live. Everything affirms that in the physical and spiritual worlds, there is, and has always been, enough.

This truth rings deep in my soul, and I am moved and motivated at a cellular level. This truth penetrates and permeates my entire essence. And it is good.

And so it is!

Practice
Go around your house and find ten items you could give away—then give them away!

Quote
Faith is a commodity that cannot be quantified, yet it is the way to an ever-flowing, prosperous life. Find your faith!

Michelle Wadleigh

Affirmation of Gratitude
Today I remember to be grateful for my body and my health as it is right NOW!

Prosperous Me, Accepting the Bounty of your Birthright!

Keep track of your daily blessings, awareness's & successes.

$8.86 Food

Nov

The fruit of the tree of God is YOU!

Day 3
Treatment

Today is the day that Spirit has made. Today is the accumulation of all good works, all good thoughts, and all good consciousness. Today I stand in total acceptance of my good as I move steadily into the experience and expression of greater prosperity and greater abundance. All old ideas are supplanted with these new and consciously chosen ideas: I am wealthy; I am a money magnet; I am a receiver of good from all directions; I stay steady on the course of greater financial success. I think and act this way.

This abundance wells up from within as the one and only Source, sources itself to me seamlessly. There is only that which is generated from within. Any thoughts to the contrary are cast out and neutralized. This is my chosen truth. This is *me*, a beautiful expression of abundance. Sensing my gratitude for the truth that is known and is my power, I do surrender this word.
And so it is!

Practice
Wise rich people have some habits in common, like: keep careful track of the money you spend daily. Keep a small pad or journal on your person to do so. You will make wiser decisions when you know what is really going on.

Quote
The spiritual substance from which comes all visible wealth is never depleted. It is right with you all the time and responds to your faith in it and your demands upon it.

Charles Fillmore

Affirmation of Gratitude
I am grateful for my home as it is right now.

Peak 0 6 @$50.00

Prosperous Me, Accepting the Bounty of your Birthright!

Keep track of your daily blessings, awareness's & successes.

$7.00   Sukyo Mahikari oct1

$18.45   Gas✓ $5.89 Food

$50.00 Reward $10.00 Tips $20.00 Gas $1.95 Coffee Nov

$7.65 Supplies $27.14 Food

Tip those who serve you generously.

Day 4
Treatment

There is one Power that moves with ease and grace. It is creative, loving, and always available. I align myself with this Power when placing my demands upon the universal law. This Power burns through any and all of my conditioned resistance. This Power sees truth where I see only confusion. This Power opens the way where I feel blocked. This Power recognizes only possibilities. This Power is My Power. This Power is Life as Me. This Power is that which lifts, drives, and moves me to the next level of expression. On this day, I accept the movement of this Power toward greater abundance in my personal life and my life as a change agent for those around me.

Today I declare that I am ready, willing, and able to succeed, prosper, and expand my expression of prosperity. Everything in the universe supports this demand NOW. I am ready, willing, and able to receive like never before. THIS IS MY TRUTH NOW!
And so it is!

Practice
Create a new and empowering habit. Each day open your mail as soon as possible, and recycle the unnecessary mail. Open the bills RIGHT AWAY, bless them, and put them in the right place to be paid on time. When you pay them, do so from a place of gratitude.

Quote
When I chased after money, I never had enough. When I got my life on purpose and focused on giving of myself and everything that arrived into my life, then I was prosperous.

Wayne Dyer

Affirmation of Gratitude
Today I value the influence of my nuclear family as they are/were!

Prosperous Me, Accepting the Bounty of your Birthright!

Keep track of your daily blessings, awareness's & successes.

$68.00   Oil chng.   10   oct.
$ 8.00   Car wash   10
$ 10.15   Gas   10
$ 2.18   Shake
$ 29.73   Flowers & Card   10
$ 4.29   Food
$3.00 Tips $34.08 Food $9.25 movie $16.85 gas   Nov   Nov

Day 5
Treatment

Keeping my focus on what's possible, I allow myself to remember that as a child of God, I am in line for my direct inheritance from my Mother/Father, provider, God. No matter what has preceded this point in time, I am able to access divine wisdom, intelligence, and the kind of inspiration that moves and motivates me past old limitations.

This spoken word is by far more powerful than any old ideas, restricting habits, or ANY identification I may have had as someone who was not available to prosperity. For in Truth there is only NOW!

I am available to new ideas that replace and supplant that which has undermined my abundance and greatness. These new ideas are all versions of: I am open to my good, worthy of my good and available to my abundant good now. Right now, I am open to having my consciousness be grown, moved, motivated, and expanded as I accept my Divine Birthright and my share of prosperity.

This is my truth, and no idea or thing can undo this word which has been spoken.
And so it is!

Practice
The next time you go out to eat, make sure you know your server's name, thank her/him for the service, and double the tip – just because!

Quote
The Universe does not compensate individuals based on the activity of work, but on the activity of consciousness.

John Randolph Price

Affirmation of Gratitude
Today I express gratitude—if only in my heart—to all of my past teachers.

Prosperous Me, Accepting the Bounty of your Birthright!

Keep track of your daily blessings, awareness's & successes.

$30.00 Fastrak   Tips $14.00
$20.00 Gas $13.50 laundry
$13.50 Gas $1.95 Coffee $28.57 Food   Mon

There is an intelligence governing your life, LISTEN!

Day 6
Treatment

It is with great enthusiasm that I begin to stalk all old and limiting ideas that might be hovering anywhere in my consciousness, in my behavior, or in my habits. Willingly, I practice radical honesty, as I peer into my mind in order to find any discord and replace ideas and beliefs that cause the discord with newer, freer, more liberating ideas.

It is downright ridiculous to consider myself unworthy of wild and wonderfully abundant good, especially knowing that as my good grows, I am always willing to share from my overflow. I am always willing to be a conduit for good. Through this practice, I increase my willingness to receive and to give abundantly. I am ready to embrace my generosity and to be a source of good for all.

This expression of generosity is born of the knowing that I have only one source, God. God gives to me and gives through me, and all who are close to me can feel this very natural flow of good. I stand poised gracefully to receive and to give. With abundant gratitude, I release this word and allow it to be so.
And so it is!

Practice

To suggest doing something kind can sound like a cliché; however, practicing random acts of kindness and generosity cultivates a pathway within that opens us up to greater good. Begin practicing random acts of kindness and generosity, but don't worry about being noticed. This is for YOU—your heart and your expansion. Others will simply benefit.

Quote

We are floating in an 'ocean' of thought-energy, where all the knowledge there ever was or ever will be, is present.

Bob Proctor

Affirmation of Gratitude

Thank you, Life, for this body temple that allows my humanness.

Confirm

$3.00 65796 0121 754785 Metro
$19.63 Food $.25 Cup $50 Valero Debt. $19.60 Gas
$ .25 Cup   Tips $18.00
$ 50.00 Valero $150 Bonus/ $15.00 Tips   NOV
$18.50 Restr. $21.50 Food $17.30 Gas $8.00 Movies NOV
$150.70 nyb

Day 7
Treatment

There is a power for good that is omnipresent, and in this moment It shows up in, through, and as my life. This is my life. No separation, not even a breath, can distance me from my God.

I recognize this total immersion with Life, with God, as the access to my good. This direct access is my truth, and it always has been, even if there are moments when I don't know it consciously. All aspects of me: my mind which is open to an expanded consciousness; my heart as it willingly opens to my good; and my soul are ready to be expressed prosperously. I am ready to find the language, to develop the habits, the know-how, and the understanding required to be prosperous now. Now I am ready for movement. Now I am ready to understand. Now I am ready to prosper in so many amazing ways. Now the goodness of life shows up on my doorstep, and the evidence is bountiful.

This shift reflecting my readiness is good, exciting, and so, so natural. It is natural for me to be abundant, and natural for me to feel *rich*. I was born to receive good. I was born to live in the abundant flow of all good. With gratitude I accept my good. And so it is!

Practice
Send thank you notes for any reason and mail them OR leave notes of thanks for people in your own home, even for things they are "supposed" to do.

Quote
If you want to succeed you should strike out on new paths, rather than travel the worn paths of accepted success.

John D. Rockefeller

Affirmation of Gratitude
I am so grateful for all the people in my life who have supported me throughout my life.

Prosperous Me, Accepting the Bounty of your Birthright!

$1.45 Coffee   TIP $2.00 Tip   Oct.
$9.00 Tips $18.40 Gas
$4.77 Water $16.36 Court
$2.10 Items $173.73 Bonus
$ .50 Prkng
$8.00 Car wsh $11.10 Gas $18.07 Food   NOV.

Day 8
Treatment

A new week, a new idea, a new level of acceptance, deeper, more open, more willing--this is my Now experience. Not only am I willing to have a shift in consciousness, I am also willing to do what is necessary to be moved to right and effective action. I am living in and from the consciousness that declares I am rich, so I behave in a powerful and responsible way.

I accept this truth: I am rich; I am a money magnet; and I am of the mind of abundance in all ways, I behave so all my affairs are in Divine order. All of my business is cared for in a responsible manner. I live in total integrity, and this leads to my income increasing more and more all the time. My income is an exciting bit of evidence that shows my shift in consciousness. The evidence surrounds me everywhere.

This is good and very good. I am moving into wild increase of income, love, joy, and health. Yay for me! Yay for me! And so it is!

Practice
Pay your smallest credit card bill first + a percentage more. When it is paid off, add this payment to your next bill and watch the snowball effect of paying your bills.

Quote
Anyone who lives within their means suffers from a lack of imagination.

Oscar Wilde

Affirmation of Gratitude
I am grateful for indoor plumbing, running water, and paved streets.

Prosperous Me, Accepting the Bounty of your Birthright!

Keep track of your daily blessings, awareness's & successes.

$17.00 Tips $33.00 Shoe Rpr
$14.45 Gas $7.83 Food
$1.95 Coffee $10.94 Phone Chrgr Cable
$.89 Food
$1.95 Coffee $13.25 Gas $12.99 Food $9.00 Tips Nov.

Life is always calling your forth, heed the call!

Day 9
Treatment

Oh what a beautiful morning it is when Life begins to show up on my doorstep, on my terms! Not accidently or by chance, but by the words of my mouth, by my declaration, by my decided mind, and by my willingness to be prospered. There is movement today in me, through me, as me. It is God and me in a dance, and a full-out celebration ensues.

I am happy to be in this dance, and I am ridiculously happy that God is my dance partner and the lead. I surrender to this dance with all the grace that I can muster. I allow myself to be pushed, pulled, and guided across life's dance floor. God dances me through the halls of possibility, of living a prosperous life. I live life full-out, wonderfully, marvelously, gracefully.

Being a willing dance partner in the responsible hands of God, I celebrate on this good and glorious day.
And so it is!

Practice
Begin to wake up earlier. Successful people don't stay in bed, they *do*! You should embrace your day with great enthusiasm and expectancy.

Quote
You are living on the precipice of possibility. Choose brilliance and the highest possibility today!

Michelle Wadleigh

Affirmation of Gratitude
I am grateful for my intelligence.

Prosperous Me, Accepting the Bounty of your Birthright!

$7.00 Tips $2.90 Food   Oct.

$2.05 Coffee $5.50 Food

$12.49 Movies $6.46 Eat Out   ↓

$7.75 Gas $5.36 Food $13.90 Gas   Nov.

Look into the mirror daily and remind yourself of your worthiness.

Day 10
Treatment

This is the day that Spirit has made using all of Its infinite resources. As I attempt to imagine that God's infinite resources coalesced to create this one beautiful moment, I am moved to an experience of total awe that takes my breath away and reminds me of my humble essence. Into this essence I melt, merge, and become one with the One.

This One wants for me so much more that I have dreamed for myself. In this now, I begin to take on the idea of all, of more, of the Infinite as It wells up from inside. The Infinite Intelligence that is, sources me all that I could dream of, multiplied by one hundred. There, right before my eyes, I am gifted with more love, more enthusiasm, more joy, more peace, more success, more money, and more overall prosperity than I ever dreamed.

My consciousness stands at the ready to be stretched and moved into an expanded position. This position is me--hands open, face up, declaring my willingness to receive all good from all directions. I am ready. I am open. I am worthy of this good and greater good.
And so it is!

Practice
Give a secret gift to a co-worker or neighbor.

Quote
Let us clothe ourselves in the great realization that all power is ours and nothing else can enter... Spirit will never fail us if we never fail to believe in Its goodness and Its responsiveness.
                                                                    Ernest Holmes

Affirmation of Gratitude
I stay conscious of my breath and grateful for its flow. It is a gift from the One.

Prosperous Me, Accepting the Bounty of your Birthright!

Keep track of your daily blessings, awareness's & successes.

$25.30 Walmart $28.00 Gas out
$13.00 Tips $150.00 Bonus ✓ $12.00 tips NOV.
$6.46 Restrnt $9.69 copy $6.95 FF $17.15 Gas $1.85 Coffee

The breath of life is breathing through you now and
it is abundant.

Day 11
Treatment

This day has catapulted me into a dimension of faith unlike anything I have known before. This day has prompted and prodded me to open, to grow, and then to remain open and to grow more. I say "Yes !" to this invitation. My yes creates my covenant with the Creator. My yes opens my mind and heart to receive so much more good than I could have possibly imagined before this moment.

The receptors in my brain are now rewiring their connections to respond to ideas of greatness. My greatness is being created, actualized, and propagated. I make good and meaningful decisions. I spend and save my money wisely. I make decisions around all the business of my life from a grounded and solid place. I am surrounded by individuals who know money intimately, and who advise me from that knowing. I am prospered from their advice.

The wisdom of the wealthy is everywhere present, and it is informing me now. I accept this good without reservation. And so it is.

Practice
Take time to research successful individuals whom you admire. Study their methods, and find inspiration in their success.

Quote
Man is just what he thinks himself to be... He will attract to himself, what he thinks most about. He can learn to govern his own destiny when he learns to control his thoughts.

Ernest Holmes

Affirmation of Gratitude
Today I am grateful for the forefathers of this country who gave me a platform to be free and fully expressed.

Prosperous Me, Accepting the Bounty of your Birthright!

$9.00 Tips $1.95 Coffee $17.25 Gas
$4.48 Target $17.93 Food $ 1.99 Food
$2.86 Food $ 1.52 Food   Oct

Nov $9.00 Tips $8.00 Cinema $18.00 car wsh $9.10 Gas $27.11 Food
$

TAKING ACTION

Many within the spiritual community can often be guilty of wanting to pray, meditate, and create vision boards but at all cost avoid doing the work that is necessary to prepare and position oneself to receive good. Sitting on your meditation pillow is fine if that is what you want, but sitting on your meditation pillow and then getting up and doing things necessary will have you feeling alive, vital, and empowered.

What to do:
- Practice gratitude by sending notes *snail mail.*
- Actively practice forgiveness for everyone, including yourself.
- Pay your bills on time.
- Return phone calls.
- Be in integrity in all places in your life.
- Empty drawers.
- Clear out chaos.
- Give away anything you haven't touched or worn in a year.
- Take care of your body; it's the only one you have.
- Get inspiration by going out into nature.
- Keep learning anything that supports your interests.
- Stay in balance within your life.
- Work from creating to-do lists to stay on target.
- Create a mastermind group.
- Keep your goals fresh in your mind by writing them out.
- Take action even if you're not ready.
- Say yes to opportunities.
- Get up early in the morning and seize the day.
- Network and contact everyone all who may support you.
- Read stories about successful people.
- Stay aware of your balances and your debt.
- Open all mail immediately, and handle everything ASAP.
- Take risks; they will grow you.
- Learn how to negotiate. Never take what is dished out.
- Be aware of your score.
- Always keep savings available for fun and taking risks.

Prosperous Me, Accepting the Bounty of your Birthright!

- Keep thinking big, keep new ideas flowing.
- Seek criticism and feedback; you will grow from it.
- Work harder that what is expected.
- Give more than what you are paid for.
- Continue to follow your passion.
- Speak kindly about all people all the time.
- Give generously of your overflow.
- Resist any temptation to gossip, complain, or judge.

Once you have invested an effectual amount of time developing your spiritual practices, including prayer and meditation, you will find yourself being pulled to live from consciousness first. You will be accessing the same wisdom and infinite genius that has been available to all those who have inspired you to reach for more.

Those who consider themselves conscious will always find the greatest satisfaction when their decision making and their actions are in alignment. You are called to move from the inside out, but moving is definitely part of the formula.

Day 12
Treatment

No problem can throw me off my Center. No issue can distract me from my good. Nothing gets my attention other than my total and complete reliance on God, the One, the only source of my good, my love, and my prosperity. No human activity is bigger than the formless creation of Good.

Today I declare once again: I accept that I am fully functioning and worthy of good. I accept my abundance beyond anything I have ever, ever known. My life as me, in all the roles that I play, is fully informed and governed by God. My good is sourcing itself to me now, right now, without delay or hesitation, acknowledging that God and only God is the source of my good. I am so incredibly grateful for what I know and for what I don't know, realizing it is all working in my favor. Ah, yes.
And so it is!

Practice
Pay for the person behind you in line at the coffee shop or the toll, or wherever you are!

Gratitude
Money, money, money manifest thyself here and now in rich abundance.

Catherine Ponder

Affirmation of Gratitude
Thank you to my challenges and my discomfort. I am grown by them.

Prosperous Me, Accepting the Bounty of your Birthright!

Keep track of your daily blessings, awareness's & successes.

$8.00 Car Wash   #18.37 Food   #11.05 Gas 8 oct
$38.00 Alteration
ov. $8.00 Tips #14.70 Gas #12.49 Cinema $6.00 FstFd $5.37 FstFood

Turn your face away from doubt and turn to Possibility.

Day 13
Treatment

      I am clear that what sometimes appears to be a test is only an opportunity for me to refine my skills. Life is the grit that polishes me into the diamond that I am. Through this process, I am pulled more and more deeply into my spiritual practices and my acceptance. There has never been a better time for life to prosper me. There has never been a more ripe and fertile time for me to accept my rightful place among those who prosper and to share from their prosperity. It is so beautiful as I allow inspiration to move and motivate me and my offerings to the world, for I know it is not I but of the presence and power of the Mother/Father/God within that does the work.

      This good is closer than my hands and feet, closer than my next breath. I am steady, sturdy, and on target. I am the calm at the center of the storm of creation, and I assume a healthy posture of readiness knowing all is well.
And so it is!

Practice
Always finish your to-do list. Get in the habit of never leaving anything incomplete at the end of the day. If you simply do what you set out to do, it will be hard for success to elude you.

Quote
Don't be afraid to let give up the good to go for the great.
John D. Rockefeller

Affirmation of Gratitude
I am grateful for the awareness of my Divine Birthright of good.

Prosperous Me, Accepting the Bounty of your Birthright!

$23.00 Tips $.25 prkng   #15.96 Food oct.

Nov. $7.00 Tips $20.00 Gas $17.47 DVD $29.40 Food

Day 14
Treatment

I live in the land and the consciousness of plenty. Plenty is my experience with all things. Plenty is how my finances show up. Plenty is how my support and financial influx shows up. Plenty is the love that I experience. Plenty is my consciousness. Plenty. Plenty. Plenty.

God is this plenty, for God as the Infinite can only give all, all the time. God cannot help but give me all my dreams, all my love, all my health, and all my prosperity. The sweet and abundant Source finds me right where I am. I was the one who was not accepting this generosity, but now I have a changed mind, a new idea, a greater sense of self, of worthiness, and of self-love. I believe that God is naturally outpouring Itself to me, and I accept.
And so it is!

Practice
Sensing a shift in consciousness? If yes, give from that feeling. Give from your shift, from your overflow. Give to the source of your inspiration. Give more love to your family and friends from this overflow. Give to strangers by looking them in the eye and seeing Spirit in them. Be a giver, and your life will always be RICH.

Quote
It takes 20 years to build a reputation and five minutes to ruin it. If you think about that, you'll do things differently.
Warren Buffett

Affirmation of Gratitude
I am so grateful for the beauty of this world. It surrounds me everywhere.

Prosperous Me, Accepting the Bounty of your Birthright!

$8.00 Tips $19.10 Gas   Kitchen $11.16
$7.83 Food $7.05 Gas $7.28 Food $4.87 Rest.   3 Oct.

Day 15
Treatment

This is the day the Lord has made. Oh, such words have never before left my mouth with such sincerity! I believe that the "Lord"/Law/Life is working in my favor as the one and only Source of all. I believe in good, in God, in love, in possibility and in being fully worthy of all that the Mother/Father/Creator ever intended for me to have.

My consciousness is growing in leaps and bounds every day. My consciousness is expanding, and through this expansion I accept my riches, my abundance, and my prosperity. It is with total conviction that I choose to believe that I reap the beautiful and direct results of the expansion of my consciousness. Not only do I reap the rewards of my consciousness, but I stand grounded in this consciousness, and as it grows it touches the lives of everyone around me. Yes, my own Field of Consciousness grows and wherever I go, It is, and It is good. It is palpable, and It is potent--truly transforming lives everywhere. I am so grateful to be one of the many who carry this vibration with me everywhere. Everyone around me is prospering now.

This is good and very good.
And so it is!

Practice
When you pay your bills, send in a thank you note with the check.

Quote
A man is not rightly conditioned until he is a happy, healthy, and prosperous being; and happiness, health, and prosperity are the result of a harmonious adjustment of the inner with the outer of the man with his surroundings.

James Allen

Affirmation of Gratitude
I am so grateful for the inspiration of the generosity I see everywhere around me in this world.

Prosperous Me, Accepting the Bounty of your Birthright!

xt $2.25 Coffee $13.75 Gas $7.88 Food $4.17 Food

ou $32.00 Tips $5.87 Food $2.90 Rest. $16.25 Gas

Life is constantly conspiring in your favor; it is its nature to do so.

Day 16
Treatment

I am so clear that God loves all of me; I am willing to risk it all. I am willing to risk more love just to love. I am willing to be wrong in order to find my "rightness." I am willing to try and try again, to find out how to do things better. I am willing to live life on the edge to find that place of creativity. Oh yes, I am willing to allow God to use me as a vessel for good and greater good.

This attitude and this consciousness lend themselves to my growth, my abundance, and my success. I stand in the declaration that I am total, obvious, and measureable success. My life and consciousness are magnets for money. My home is in good and wonderful order. My career is a perfect complement to my desires and is hugely successful. My creative self-expression is constantly evolving and reflecting my most freely expressed self. This is all made possible because I am willing to take the risk of SUCCEEDING!

Feeling loved, guided, and informed by God, I release this word into Law.
And so it is.

Practice
Today, see how many compliments you can give away. Pay attention to everyone and everything around you, and catch as many people as you can doing something wonderful.
Remember to thank individuals for things they do all the time. Big and little things deserve the same recognition.

Quote
As much as we need a prosperous economy, we also need prosperity of kindness and decency.

Caroline Kennedy

Affirmation of Gratitude
I am grateful for the kindness that I see everywhere in this world.

Prosperous Me, Accepting the Bounty of your Birthright!

$6.46 Food $8.85 Gas $9.86 Supplies
$2.05 Gas $ .85 Food $10.97 Food
Oct $10.97 Food
Nov $68.00 oil $15.04 Gas $12.45 Food

Try asking yourself this: Why not me?

Day 17
Treatment

Life is my source. Life is my one source. Life is my one and only source. Nothing that happens around me can distract me from this truth. I am always guided and informed by this **Intelligence**. All that Life knows that applies to me, is known through me. This is good and very, very good. I am never outside of Life. I am never outside of the arms of Life, the thinking of Life, or the love of Life. Life is my heart, my mind, my soul.

Experiencing this truth at the very core of my being, I am always inspired, moved, and motivated by this Intelligence. My dreams are fully inspired. My business decisions are grounded, logical, and intelligent. As I build my consciousness, my actions are driven from that expanded consciousness. I never confuse being busy with being effective. Each day begins and ends with my spiritual practice which keeps me plugged into this flow of guidance.

I am a prospering human of high inspiration, intellect, and bountiful success in ALL ENDEAVORS. Everything I touch prospers NOW! This is my truth, and no other truth is more important or more real than this. This is known deep in my subconscious. This is known in my all-conscious. This is WHO I AM! And so it is!

Practice
Stop being quiet about your desires. Create a mastermind group into which you can speak your desires loudly, boldly, and with total authority. You must feel the impact of your own goals, or you won't move a single muscle.

Quote
Thought is the only power which can produce tangible riches from the Formless Substance. The stuff from which all things are made is a substance which thinks. And the very thought of a form in this substance produces that form.

Wallace Wattles

Affirmation of Gratitude
I am grateful for how Intelligence demonstrates in my life each and every day.

Prosperous Me, Accepting the Bounty of your Birthright!

Keep track of your daily blessings, awareness's & successes.

$1.95 Coffee $11.30 Gas $8.00 Gas $15.01 Food

NOV $3.27 Rest.

Remember to give from your overflow in a generous way.

Day 18
Treatment

Today I experience the full measure my gratitude for all aspects of my life, without exception. I accept that all parts of my life are constantly working in my favor, working for me, working around me, working for me to my highest, freest, and most prosperous expression always.

This good happens not because of any effort on my part, but because the one Source and Supply of all good as it is forever expressing Itself, and I am simply one of Its available vessels through which it expresses fully.

I am so incredibly grateful for all that has preceded this moment and for the experiences that have refined my way of being. I am grateful for my wins and for my perceived losses as they have all supported my transformation. I am grateful for all the people who are in, or who have passed through, my life. I am grateful for God as my One and only Source of Inspiration, Abundance and Prosperity. Today *I am my gratitude*, for it is the vibration that I am.
And so it is!

Practice
It is time in this series to talk about the effect of forgiveness on prosperity. Holding on to upset, resentment, and blame is one of the most destructive habits. Until we free ourselves from holding ill feelings, we run the risk of staying stuck, of holding on to the weight of the world, and of not allowing ourselves to be in the flow. Forgive so that you may live in the prosperous flow of life.

Quote
When we step out of the shadow of this distorted and outdated system and the mind-set it generates, what we discover is this: Scarcity is a lie.

Lynne Twist

Affirmation of Gratitude
I am grateful for every thought, every feeling, and every life experience.

Prosperous Me, Accepting the Bounty of your Birthright!

Keep track of your daily blessings, awareness's & successes.

$17.15 Gas $1.95 coffee $7.83 Food
Nov $12.35 Gas $7.15 Past $8.00 wash

Deep within there is a fount that sources itself in proportion to your receptivity.

Day 19
Treatment

On this day I am grateful for my family, my friends, and all the people who have ever populated my life. I am grateful for my ancestry and for my ability to relate to it or not. I am grateful for all that has come before this moment. I am grateful for my good and my not-so-good. I am equally grateful for ease and grace and for the appearance of struggle. I am grateful for every breath and every thought. Each and every moment I invest in my gratitude is a moment of expanding my consciousness. This investment expands my consciousness and fertilizes the soil of my being to accept more and more abundance all the time.

Ideas flow out of me because of this attitude of gratitude. Money-making ideas find me right where I am, and all the talent that God affords me prospers me now. I am totally prepared to generate more and more money on the human level, for I know that Spirit is the one and only power that is powering me up right now.
And so it is!

Practice
Keep an active idea journal. Write down all ideas with equal enthusiasm. You will be guided by your inspired intelligence which ideas to serve and which to leave behind.

Quote
If you fix upon your consciousness that fact that the desire you feel for the possession of riches is one with the desire of Omnipotence for more complete expression, your faith becomes invincible.
Wallace Wattles.

Affirmation of Gratitude
I take this moment to thank the *wanting* that has led me to having.

Prosperous Me, Accepting the Bounty of your Birthright!

Keep track of your daily blessings, awareness's & successes.

ct $ $27.00 Tips #61.79 clothes #12.50 Gas #1.95 coffee
$ 7.37 Food
100 $12.00 Tips $15.35 Gas #14.32 food #2.90 Rest $10.99 movies

Be prosperous is not difficult, it is as easy as breathing.

Day 20
Treatment

There is only One Life. This Life is beautiful, powerful, always available, always creating out of Itself. It is always wherever I am, in whatever I think, and in all decisions that I make. This Life is my life NOW. WOW!

I am open to the influence and inspiration of this One Source. At the deepest part of my subconscious, I am open to growing, glowing, and having all the thoughts necessary to have expanded life and ever-expanding prosperity.

Anything that might still hover in my subconscious, and might stand in the way, is now uprooted and gone. What takes its place are new, more empowering ideas of great prosperity and abundance. This is the truth. This is my truth. This is who I am. And so it is!

Practice
Find a few minutes every day to brainstorm and to experience the vibration that gets activated when you invest time in creative imagining. Don't attach yourself to any one idea. The purpose is to cultivate your creativity. Create that you may live creatively.

Quote
Nothing but lack of faith can keep my good from me, for I am one with the Universal Essence of Life, or Spirit, and Its Substance will manifest in my experience as I believe.

Ernest Holmes

Affirmation of Gratitude
I am grateful for the fount of inspiration that lives within me.

Prosperous Me, Accepting the Bounty of your Birthright!

Keep track of your daily blessings, awareness's & successes.

Ct $20.00 Gas $18.00 Car Wsh $21.61 Food
Tax. $4.00 Tips $6.23 $19.75 Gas $2.10 Coffee

Trust your intuition: you are smarter than you think.

RECEPTIVITY

Have you ever found yourself observing individuals who seem to have life working for them on their behalf? As you watch them--the way they move, speak, make decisions or even walk into a room--you can see that it is natural for them to take full dominion over their lives, to graciously handle the attention when they enter a room, and to accept the good that comes to them in all forms.

We have all witnessed this kind of person and for many; this observation will spark feelings of jealousy, envy, competition or being less than. What do they have? Who are they? Why is it so easy for them to say yes and accept their good and their blessed good. The reason? They believe they deserve their good, and they are willing to receive the abundance that the Spirit has bestowed upon them as their Divine Birthright. *This same Birthright is your right also*. It is imperative that you cultivate the consciousness and the willingness to receive.

In order to heighten your receptivity, be on the lookout for any belief in doubt, fear, lack, limitation or idea that you do not deserve your good. Be on the lookout for any messages you adopted consciously or absorbed from everywhere around you. Catch each thought as you discover it, give it no more time to become any more real then it already has. Each and every time you catch even an inkling of one of these beliefs, right in that moment affirm: *This is not my truth. This not who I am.*

Your truth is this: I am a child of the Most High, born to be fully expressed in every way, and I am willing to receive my full measure of good. I stand tall and ready, turning my hands up in a posture to receive. As I do, heaven pours its good over me, and in return, I give from my overflow. Yes, I am willing to receive more love and more prosperity than ever.

I walk in the consciousness of prosperity.
I act from the consciousness of prosperity. I am the consciousness of prosperity.

Day 21
Treatment

Speaking into the Mind and Power that is everywhere present, always available, and always saying yes, I declare for myself right NOW, that I am fully, fully, fully supported in many different and abundant ways. The Thing Itself believes in ME. And I know this because even the very impulse of Spirit urges me to open and receive in proportion to my Divine Birthright. Expert guidance and support are constantly sourced to me from this Intelligence in all categories that matter in support of my developing expression. By the effectiveness of the Power that has invested Itself in me, and by use of the spoken and written word, lives all around me are changed and transformed for the better forever, beginning with my own. This happens because only truth is spoken. It is God's truth, and God's word and worth will not be denied.

I am a carrier of good. I give generously of this good, and I receive in greater proportion than my giving. This word is good and very good.
And so it is!

Practice
Every day seek to serve, to be generous, to give, to compliment, and to bless. Every day there is, be the blessing in the room. Be the one who finds the silver lining. Be the one who is forgiving and compassionate. Hold the door, let that next car in, tip a bit more, and call your family. Yes, BE THE BLESSING. Make this your intention until it is your natural way of being.

Quote
Give every man more in use value than you take from him in cash value; then you are adding to the life of the world by every business transaction.

Wallace Wattles

Affirmation of Gratitude
I am so incredibly grateful for the good that I see each and every time that I open my eyes. This good blesses me always.

Prosperous Me, Accepting the Bounty of your Birthright!

Keep track of your daily blessings, awareness's & successes.

$24.00 Tips $43.50 Vitamins $1.95 Coffee $800 Movie
($13.30 Gas OCt) $7.00 Tips $4.24 Food
Nov.

There is no Source separate from you, it is within.

Day 22
Treatment

There is One Life; that Life is Good; that Life is God; that Life is my Life now. This One Good Life is filled with such amazing love and inspiration, and it is always sourcing itself to me, through me, and *as* me.

This inspiration gives of itself generously. I am inspired to create beauty all around me, and I share this beauty freely. This beauty opens hearts, opens doors, and opens up my creative life. Yes, I surrender totally to this creativity, to intelligence, and to the life of God. I surrender to the highest call, and I listen for that call. I recognize the intuition that would have its way with me, and I live in the divine covenant of YES. This is the Truth; this is my Truth; this is that which opens up and activates greatness within me. With this movement comes great prosperity, for the flow that is happening is powerful. I am prospered so I may continue to be a conduit for good for years to come.

I accept this Truth now as I experience a deeply resounding sense of gratitude for Law, for Love, and for Awe. The place where these things dwell within me is my constant source of good. And so it is!

Practice
Tithe to the source of your inspiration – even if it is NOT a tax write-off.

Quote
Ideas are the beginning points of all fortunes. Ideas are products of the imagination.

Napoleon Hill

Affirmation of Gratitude
I am grateful to the place where Spirit dwells within and how It guides me toward right action always.

Prosperous Me, Accepting the Bounty of your Birthright!

Keep track of your daily blessings, awareness's & successes.

$16.00 Tips $12.80 Gas $13.52 food $2.05 coffee MON
$15.00 Gas $1.40 Past $3.58 Supplies $17.89 foods

Imagine yourself being in the flow each and every day. Make it vivid.

Day 23
Treatment

There is One. This One is my I AM. This One I AM is beautiful, potent, and Its reach is far and deep. Deep within me and far within all that is. I remain consciously available to it, open to all of its magnificent and meticulous influence.

After being reminded so many times by so many sources, I choose to believe with all my might and heart that the Creator of this incredible world has always intended for each of us to prosper abundantly. So today I say out loud: I ACCEPT! I ACCEPT MY GOOD, MY ABUNDANCE, MY PROSPERITY AND THE FULL MEASURE OF MY BIRTHRIGHT.

I declare that my subconscious mind is completely on board to accept these seeds of change. I declare that this is who I am and how I function. This is good and very good. It is who I am. I accept enthusiastically this Truth and the truth that there is only one Source, It is everywhere present and there is *no* source other than this one Source. I live in profound gratitude as this Source moves through me and my life now!
And so it is!

Practice
Every time the phone rings, BEFORE ANSWERING IT, breathe and say: *I accept my good and my greater good.* Make this a permanent habit.

Quote
Prosperity is the out-picturing of substance in our affairs. Everything in the Universe is for us. Nothing is against us. We must know that everywhere we go we meet friendship, love, human interest, and helpfulness. Life is ever giving of Itself. We must receive, utilize, and extend the gift.

Ernest Holmes

Affirmation of Gratitude
I am grateful for all who have gone before me offering wisdom and inspiration that has expanded my life experience.

Prosperous Me, Accepting the Bounty of your Birthright!

$12.25 Gas $1.95 Coffee $18.29 food $10.00 Tips
$113.11 Supplies (Mou) $9.00 Tips $8.00 crWsh
$10.92 food $23.15 Rest $1.95 Coffee $2.79 food

All that is beautiful, abundant and lavish is available to you.

Day 24
Treatment

Right here and right now, as I focus my attention on feeling worthy, I can hear the almost imperceptible whisper reminding me to love and accept myself exactly as I am. Because I am a child of the Creator, I deserve my good. I remember my Truth, for it is God's Truth, and God's Truth demands to be seen, spoken about, and actualized. God's Truth is that I am capable and worthy of all good, all forgiveness, all greatness, all knowledge, all skills. I am deserving of good, love, and abundance beyond my wildest dreams.

Any appearance of struggle is only a feeling, a human measurement, and in no way determines My Truth. I am open and available to good that moves above and beyond my wildest dreams. Good is my natural state, and it is of highest influence in my life now and forever. Good is My Truth and my inspiration, and because of it, money comes to me in all forms, from all places, because it is good. Financial success is guaranteed to me now and always, and every molecule of my being accepts this truth, this reality, because it is good.

With abundant gratitude, I release this word and allow it to be so.
And so it is!

Practice

Create a blueprint for yourself, or as some like to call it, a vision board. Make your board vibrant with photos. Remember, your mind needs mental equivalents (spiritual prototypes) to create. So provide photos that spark your mind's willingness to receive.

Quote

No matter the distraction, no matter the appearance, let nothing capture your attention away from knowing that your Divine Birthright is absolute love, total health, and eternal creativity and prosperity.

Michelle Wadleigh

Affirmation of Gratitude

I am grateful for good that flows into my life like water flowing so naturally to any vessel that will receive it.

Prosperous Me, Accepting the Bounty of your Birthright!

Keep track of your daily blessings, awareness's & successes.

$8.00 Tips $20.00 Gas $2.05 coffee $4.16 Food
ov. $9.00 Tips $1.95 coffee $13.30 food $15.50 Gas

The Intelligence that created heaven and earth, created YOU!

Day 25
Treatment

Life is so good, so vibrant, and oh so juicy! On this beautiful day, I begin to pay attention to the world around me. I invest a portion of my time and attention knowing that my good is from the One Good and that all beings deserve this same measure of good. I utilize my newfound prosperity and abundance to know this for all humans everywhere. I am the example of abundance, prosperity, and generosity for myself, my family, and the world. I accept this charge for I know that in order to be a giver; I must be the possessor of good, of abundance, of prosperity. I cannot give away what I do not first possess.

I celebrate this good with every step I take, and I know that when people see me, they see Principle. I move into the responsibility of carrying this consciousness wherever I go and stand in it proudly and consciously.

Allowing myself to be prospered always by the natural, ceaseless source of abundance, I surrender this word.
And so it is!

Practice
Remember to be in your spiritual practice daily. Speak a spiritual mind treatment daily with great faith and enthusiasm.

Quote
Money is an affect. When you concentrate on the effect, you are forgetting the cause, and when you forget cause, the effect begins to diminish.

John Randolph Price

Affirmation of Gratitude
Today I celebrate the beauty of this world and all of its people, and I am moved to gratitude for the beautiful tapestry that we are.

Prosperous Me, Accepting the Bounty of your Birthright!

Keep track of your daily blessings, awareness's & successes.

$6.00 Tips $1.95 Coffee $17.00 Gas $81.34 Shoes
$15.58 Food (Nov) $5.00 Tips $12.45 Gas $7.67 Books
$1.95 Coffee $5.48 Supplies $1.70 Rest. $19.23 Food

Day 26
Treatment

Today I rest in the One. I breathe easy today, and I celebrate because I have invested time and energy in shifting my consciousness. I am grateful to stand upon the shoulders of the wisest of the wise and the work that they have brought forth to benefit humankind.

Because I have been diligent over my mind and my attention, and can sense a shift that has taken place deep within my being, I know my life is a gift worthy of great celebration. Every time I look in the mirror I see the *Me* that I choose to be. I see the strength, courage, and tenacity of one who co-creates her own good. And now, after so much work, I begin to rest, to be at ease, and to take on the attitude of gentleness and allowance. Yes, I begin to allow Life to work for me in my favor with total ease and grace; and I am never tempted to force anything into place.

My job is *what*, Spirit's job is *how*. Knowing this, I leave Spirit's job up to Spirit and let my imagination create a wild and expressive dream for myself.

I breathe a sigh of ease, and, yes, I let this be so.
And so it is!

Practice
Every night before you go to sleep, praise yourself for your good works. You deserve the praise as much as anyone.

Quote
Don't worry when you are not recognized, but strive to be worthy of recognition.

Abraham Lincoln

Affirmation of Gratitude
I am grateful for my good and my pain equally; for my clarity and my confusion equally; and for my wanting and my having equally.

Keep track of your daily blessings, awareness's & successes.

$15.00 Tips $1.00 Prkng $33.00 clothes $1.95 Coffee
$20.08 food $10.75 Gas $33.79 Pants $13.45 food
$8.00 car wash (Mov) $27.27 Supplies $2.05 Coffee $19.00 Gas
$9.09 fred

Day 27
Treatment

I am surrounded, supported, lifted, and guided always by the One. This One is always available, always within reach as It gives to me in full measure. I speak my word with boldness, greatness and confidence. Confidence *of* God, not *in* God. This confidence penetrates and permeates every cell of my body temple and allows me the luxury of experiencing my God-given worthiness. Yes, I am worthy of all good, all the time. This shows up in ways expected and unexpected, from avenues known and new. I live in full celebration of the boundless flow of good that comes in and through my life with total ease and grace.

This is not something that I need to create, because it already is. I call forth into my life the most beautiful unfolding of the miraculous in every way possible. I stand at the ready and I am willing as always to accept my good and my greater good.
And so it is!

Practice
KEEP YOUR PROMISES TO YOURSELF as much as you would keep your promise to anyone you love.

Quote
A person's worth is measured by the worth of what he values.
Marcus Aurelius

Affirmation of Gratitude
Thank you to every teacher of prosperity for opening my eyes to what's possible.

Prosperous Me, Accepting the Bounty of your Birthright!

I am healthy, wealthy, wise, living creative and Joy-Filled

All of my life is an example of life working

Daily, I remain plugged in and passionate about life

I give of my good and I accept all of it, now

$2.00 Tips $12.96 Food $15.15 Gas $6.01 Toiletries
$1.95 Coffee $28.00 cleaners $26.79 Supplies (NOV) $11.85 Gas
$1.95 coffee $1.70 Rest $2.25 Supplies $12.12 Food $23.00 Tips
N. $3.79 Supplies $4.02 Rest

Day 28
Treatment

As the month comes to a close, I offer you this prayer from
Ernest Holmes.

"I, (your name), know that God is the source of all supply and that
money is God in action. I know that my Good is here now. I am so
rich and so full that I have an abundance of money to spare and share
today and always. I know that true prosperity includes perfect health,
perfect wealth, and perfect happiness.
These words, which I speak in faith, now activate universal law, and
I bless the increase. And I know that I now prosper in every way. I
give thanks for this Good, and so it is!"
And so it is!

Practice
Become a joyful giver. Find more and more places and ways to give.
Let yourself become known as a generous person, and let that
reputation precede you into the room. This will open every door
before you. This is how you cultivate the law of reciprocity and keep
it flowing. Live life from YOUR overflow!

Quote
Live well and prosper.

Spock

Affirmation of Gratitude
Thank you Mother/Father/God for the ceaseless way in which you
open my heart and remind me of my greatness.

Prosperous Me, Accepting the Bounty of your Birthright!

Keep track of your daily blessings, awareness's & successes. $16.44 Calendar

$12.00 Tips #14.50 Gas $1.95 Coffee $23.12 Food Oct

$10.25 Food $14.75 Gas $1.95 Coffee Nov.

Be the one who cultivates a consciousness of possibility.

Sat

Day 29
Treatment

As my journey continues into the deep of the deep, I can sense the shift in which I have been investing my time. Yes, deep in the places where doubt and fear used to exist, I am now experiencing profound faith--the faith of God, of Good, of the natural order of this powerful universe. Each day I am reminded in a thousand different ways that God, Spirit, Life, Energy seeks to create out of Itself and to be in full expression. My job is to stand still enough while keeping my mind open and available, and I stand in a posture of open receptivity. I communicate my availability to the abundance of this universe and know that It wants to pour Itself into me.

I no longer live in the question of worthiness, for I have transcended the absurdity of this idea. I no longer wonder if my consciousness is good enough, for now I know with great certainty that I was born enough, have always been enough, and will leave this earth as ENOUGH. No more wondering and hoping. Now, there is only total and complete acceptance from the deepest crevices of my consciousness. I see worthiness and good everywhere I look and in everyone I meet, and I know that all people in all places are worthy of good and greater good. As I expand my prosperity consciousness, I become one with the solution for the world at large. This is good and very good!

And so it is!

Practice
Bless the wealth and success of everyone you see who has what you "think you want." Remember, life is not always as it seems.

Quote
The opportunity for self-expression and compensation is always open to me and I am at all times compelled to know, accept and operate upon this opportunity. I have abundance because I am abundance. 'All that the Father hath is mine.'

Ernest Holmes

Affirmation of Gratitude
Thank you for my expansion of consciousness.

Prosperous Me, Accepting the Bounty of your Birthright!

$17.00 Gas $6.08 Food $13.35 Food $8.86 Supplies
$1.95 Coffee $3.00 Tips(Nov)$17.00 Tips $12.20 Gas
$14.94 Food $8.00 Car wash $1.70 Rest $16.65 Gas

Day 30
Treatment

The One Mind is recognizing me now in a way that is different from ever before in my life. The One which is always seeking expression sees my availability as I have created it through my daily practice of surrender and declaration. Oh yes, with celebration in my heart and a moment-to-moment practice of gratitude for All of Life, I joyfully accept this shift, the spiritual shift, and the shift in my prosperity and all forms of abundance. This abundance is working in my life to create ease, grace, beauty, and riches, and I give from my newfound overflow. I give as the next natural step in the ever-expanding flow of Good, for I know that in order for this shift in my consciousness to stay alive and well, I must give to keep the flow alive. And so, I do so willingly, enthusiastically.

Oh, glorious day as my heart rejoices because the joy of co-creation has entered my life in such a powerful way! I set my sight on this way of being, and now it is alive and well at a cellular level. Yes, I have re-calibrated my mind and my being to know myself as PROSPEROUS ME. This re-calibration doesn't stop because these treatments have come to a close. Once set in motion and allowed, God continues to have Its way with me, and it is a good and beautiful thing. I am so grateful to be called to this shift, for I know that as a prosperous being, I bring more good in word and works to the world at large.

To the place in me where Spirit resides I remain always grateful.
And so it is!

Practice
Give every day--a phone call, a card, an anonymous daily gift--just like manna falls from heaven on a daily basis.

Quote
Today is the most glorious day of my life!

Michelle Wadleigh

Affirmation of Gratitude
I am grateful for the sweetness and the strength in my heart that has me show up as a spiritual warrior of truth.

Prosperous Me, Accepting the Bounty of your Birthright!

Keep track of your daily blessings, awareness's & successes.

#16.00 Tips $19.75 Gas $2.05 Coffee $24.17 food

Let your breath be a reminder of the world of plenty that you live in.

Day 31
Treatment

Dear God,

I want to express my gratitude for my life and for the place that God occupies in my life. Today I recognize that even the lack that I once felt was a gift, for it forced me to reach a truth within me which was available yet hidden from my consciousness. I am grateful for all of life's trials and tribulations because I was inspired to become more. This more is the non-local me, the one who has stopped trying to figure everything out on my own, who has learned to stop trying to do God's job (which I couldn't do on my best day at the level of my humanity). I accept the lift, the expansion, the movement to a higher expression, and I am willing to continue to be available for more. God as Me is a beautiful thing. God as Me is fun. God as Me is pure joy. God as Me is abundance in obvious and not-so-obvious ways.

From the purest place within my heart, I extend my gratitude and commit on this day to live fearlessly, faithfully, abundantly, generously while always remembering that I am one with the ONE. That which I call PROSPEROUS ME is the totality of my being. This is so now and forever.
And so it is!

Practice
Treat, pray, read, and count your blessings every single day!

Quote
There is a Power for Good in the Universe and you can use it.
Ernest Holmes

Affirmation of Gratitude
Today I am grateful to myself and my willingness to grow and to succeed.

Prosperous Me, Accepting the Bounty of your Birthright!

Keep track of your daily blessings, awareness's & successes.

$6.00 Tips $20.00 Gas $1.95 Coffee $8.72 food
$1.90 Auto Rpr

You were born rich, accept your birthright!

AFTERTHOUGHT
Lack is a dis-ease

Lack is a dis-ease that is worthy of the time and attention of all metaphysicians. It is an effect of the collective consciousness of our culture, and it is the cause for much pain and suffering. The implications of lack are so much more far reaching then you might imagine. It is so much more than not having enough money, not being able to pay bills, or having a poor credit score.

Lack is so much about *our (the collective)* consciousness and how it permeates and penetrates so many of the socio-economic classes. A belief in lack tears down our self-esteem and sense of worthiness, causing a sense of desperation in the hearts and minds of millions of individuals. It is destructive in a way that goes unseen and undiagnosed until the fruit of this thinking shows up as a sense of total powerlessness.

Lack resides at a cellular level and causes some of our young men and women to make horrible, desperate decisions moving them into a corner, with their backs up against the wall, thinking the only way out is crime. The problem with this level of lack is the insidious way that it enters our communities and is passed from generation to generation.

Lack is not just a *poor man's disease*; it penetrates all levels of society. At the upper socio-economic levels, it shows up as greed. Greed is born out of lack. It is the fear of not having enough, and it is as much a lack of faith in Spirit as provider as it is being poor.

Lack must be handled from the highest level of our collective consciousness. All men and women who are awake, who know what is possible, who have read this book through to this page, who consider themselves metaphysicians must answer the call to know a new truth for all of humanity.

This problem will never be solved at the local level of charity; it must happen at the level of raising the consciousness of the planet. We who consider ourselves awake are called to know in consciousness that all people in all places are in full realization of their true Divine Birthright. Each of us was born with the right to happiness, health, love, creative expression, and prosperity.

Prosperous Me, Accepting the Bounty of your Birthright!

LET US KNOW THIS TOGETHER:

There is one great Cause. It is beautiful, powerful, and takes the names of many and the form of everything. It permeates everything, everywhere and it the cause of good.

I choose right now to believe that Cause is forming Itself in this moment as right action and right activity. In this moment I cease believing in lack. Anywhere it has existed in my consciousness and my subconscious mind is now uprooted and cast out, clearing the way for a brand new possibility.

Within this new possibility, I choose to believe in wealth in all forms, in all places, available to all people beginning within me here and now. I see through the eyes of prosperity and abundance. I act generously from this consciousness and I propagate the world with seeds of believing in the full demonstration of wealth and prosperity in my life and the lives of all people.

I see good everywhere and believe in good everywhere. I act according to a consciousness of my own worthiness as I accept my Divine Birthright as natural and right. I am fruit of the tree of possibility with strength and intelligence and great discernment. With this essence that infiltrates my being, I act as a reminder of wealth and possibility as I engage the world.

I hold the consciousness of wealth for my own life, for my family, for my community, and for my entire spiritual global family. I am the very consciousness of Prosperity.

I have abundant gratitude for this consciousness and this reality, and I surrender into it with all of my being. May good prevail for all people now and always.

And so it is!

About the Author

Reverend Michelle Wadleigh is the founding Spiritual Director of the Center for Spiritual North Jersey. She began her journey under the tutelage of Rita Sperling, a true spiritual teacher. Born in Jersey City, Rev. Michelle grew up in the suburbs of New York City but is a Jersey girl through and through. She is filled with enthusiasm, profound love, compassion and a personality that is driven to support others in their greatness.

Michelle is a coach, speaker, and workshop and retreat facilitator. She has recorded two CDs: *Organic Visioning*, and *I AM Awake*. She is the author of two other books: *40 Days to Freedom: A Lenten Practice for the Modern Mind* with Rev. Alice Reid and *And So It Is: Meditations for the Modern Mind,* a book written for the non-god centric people of the world.

Along with a large group of enthusiastic supporters, she founded the Center for Spiritual Living North Jersey in 2002, while raising the youngest of her three sons. A proud mom, Michelle brings her sensitivity for family and parenting to her ministry.

She is a practical, logical teacher, grounded in solid metaphysical principles, who brings to her teaching a wide-open heart along with a sense of humor joyfully demonstrated through her laughter. Her focus in her ministry is spiritual and emotional liberation through the application of the Science of Mind teaching. She is a straight shooter and calls things as she sees them. The lesson that she brings everywhere: **Raise your self-love quotient**.

Michelle is also the co-founder of Real Living Concepts along with Neil Pinkman, an educational organization dedicated to inspiring individuals to *master a fully expressed life;* and the creator of Radical Release Method, a form of inquiry used to identify the root cause of discord that allows practitioners to serve their clients in a powerful way.

May your life be filled with grace and joy!

Next book in the works:
Where Two or More are Gathered
Celebrating and promoting prayer partnership with instructions for treating in a powerful way.

Prosperous Me, Accepting the Bounty of your Birthright!

Made in the USA
San Bernardino, CA
22 September 2016